Not What I Expected

When Life Doesn't Turn Out as You Expected:
A Study of Exodus 16:3

F. Wayne Mac Leod

Light To My Path Book Distribution
Sydney Mines, N.S. CANADA B1V 1Y5

Not What I Expected

A Special thanks to Diane Mac Leod for proof reading this text.

Table of Contents

Preface 1
Chapter 1 - Introduction and Context 3
Chapter 2 - Life is Not Easy 9
Chapter 3 - The Unsatisfied Flesh 15
Chapter 4 - The Harshness of the Healing 23
Chapter 5 - The People in My Life 31
Chapter 6 - Faith in God's Purpose 39
Chapter 7 - Conclusion and Application 47

PREFACE

If we are honest with ourselves, life has not always turned out as we expected. As youth we imagined life with great ambition and romance. The fairy tale that was to be our life, however, was shattered by reality. Life has a way of bringing us many surprises and changing courses on us.

The nation of Israel also had their ideas of what freedom from the bondage of Egypt would look like. They had their notions of what God would do for them. Instead, they ended up in the wilderness wondering where their next meal would come from. They faced uncertainties, difficulties and disappointments. These things were not what they had anticipated. This was not their concept of freedom.

Exodus 16:3 is a simple verse that has a lot to tell us about the attitude of Israel to God and her situation. Beyond this, however, it is a powerful lesson to us as we face the disappointments and detours of life. The verse ultimately challenges us to trust God who leads us step by step through these valleys.

I have been blessed as I have followed the leading of the Lord to write on this verse. I am so thankful to the Lord for directing me to this passage of Scripture and for the insights He gave as I wandered blindly into this project. I trust that the verse will be opened up for you in a way that will bless and encourage you in the times when life does not turn out as you expected.

God bless,

F. Wayne Mac Leod

Chapter 1 - Introduction and Context

> 2 And the whole congregation of the people of Israel grumbled against Moses and Aaron in the wilderness, 3 and the people of Israel said to them, "Would that we had died by the hand of the LORD in the land of Egypt, when we sat by the meat pots and ate bread to the full, for you have brought us out into this wilderness to kill this whole assembly with hunger." (Exodus 16)

In the course of this study, I would like to take a look at these two verses of Scripture. In particular, I would like to examine the attitude of Israel toward God and their priorities in life. To be honest, when the Lord led me to this passage I wasn't sure what He wanted me to see in it. As I took the time to meditate on it, I discovered that it is a passage the looks deeply into the heart and soul of the nation of Israel. If we let the Lord speak to us through it, it may very well reveal our heart and soul as well.

Before proceeding to the verses themselves, let's examine the context in which they were written. Exodus 2:23 describes the situation the nation of Israel found themselves in at this time.

> 23 During those many days the king of Egypt died, and the people of Israel groaned because of their slavery and cried out for help. Their cry for rescue from slavery came up to God. (Exodus 2)

These were very difficult days for the people of Israel. They had been reduced to slavery in the land of Egypt. Notice how Exodus 2:23 says that the people "groaned because of their slavery." This slavery was a bitter experience. Exodus 3 recounts how the Israelites were forced to gather straw to make bricks for the construction projects of Pharaoh. Foremen were set over them to push them to meet their daily quota of bricks. If the quota was not met that day, these foremen were beaten by the Egyptian taskmasters (see Exodus 5:13-14). We can imagine that if these foremen were beaten for not producing the daily quota, then they would be pushing those under them very hard. The conditions became so intolerable that even when God sent a deliverer in the person of Moses, the people did not listen to him because their spirit had been broken:

> 9 Moses spoke thus to the people of Israel, but they did not listen to Moses, because of their broken spirit and harsh slavery. (Exodus 6)

God sent His servants, Moses and Aaron, to rescue Israel from this terrible oppression. Exodus 7-12 recounts what happened in the land of Egypt as the Lord God moved on behalf of His people. Ten plagues were released on Egypt. Those plagues destroyed the land and its crops, made life unbearable for the Egyptians and culminated in the death of the first born of every family in the nation. Only then were the people of Israel allowed to leave the land of their bondage.

As the people of God left, the Egyptians, happy to see them go, showered them with riches (see Exodus 12:33-36). The Lord led these Israelites through the desert by placing a cloudy pillar in the sky that they could follow (Exodus 13:21-22). It wasn't long before Pharaoh regretted allowing the people of Israel to leave. Gathering his army, he pursued them to the desert. He trapped them in a place of no escape, but God opened a pathway through the Red Sea. When the Egyptian army pursued them, God drowned then in the sea (Exodus 14).

There are a number of details I would like to underline here in this introduction. In those days God revealed Himself in a very special way to the people of Israel. There are six things Israel saw God do at that time.

First, Israel saw God answer their prayers. They cried out to God in their misery and the Lord heard their cry. He spoke to Moses and brought him to Egypt to be the deliverer of His people. Israel watched God answer their prayer by bringing Moses and Aaron to speak on their behalf.

Second, the people of Israel watched God judge the nation that had reduced them to slavery. The mighty God of Israel, in answer to their prayer, came to their defence. He reduced Egypt to ruins, destroyed their crops and slaughtered their firstborn children. I am sure that Israel watched in awe as they saw the anger of God on their behalf.

Third, Israel watched God set them free from a bondage they had no earthly hope of escaping. They likely had settled in their mind that this would be their lot in life and how they would live and die. God changed that, however. He set them free from the bondage of Egypt and gave them a whole new life as free people under Him.

Four, the nation of Israel watched God provide for their every need. As they left the land of bondage, they asked the Egyptians for provisions. The Lord gave them favour with the Egyptians and they gave generously so that these poor slaves were enriched with all they needed for the journey in the desert. This was something they could never have dreamed of. How could they have imagined that one day they would be enriched by their enemies. This was the work of God.

Five, God's people watched God lead them step by step through the desert. Before them every day was a pillar of cloud and fire in the sky. All they had to do was follow that pillar. The desert was a big place and they didn't know where they were going. God, however, did not leave them. The people of God watched God lead them every day. They knew His presence and direction every step of the way.

Finally, Israel watched God protect them. When the army of Egypt pursued and caught up with them at the Red Sea, God opened up the sea in a miraculous way. He allowed His people to pass over on dry land but when the Egyptian army followed, the Lord drowned them in the sea. Israel saw that the Lord God had not abandoned them. They understood by this that their God would protect and keep them all the way.

It is quite clear as we come to Exodus 16 that the Lord God had revealed Himself to Israel in a very special way. There could be no doubt that their God had come to their defence and answered their prayers in a way they had never imagined. He had proven Himself to be the God of justice who provided, protected and watched over His people. While the facts were undeniable, all too often, however, their reaction to those facts was not what it should have been. We often find ourselves in similar situations where our response to God is not as it should be. In the course of the next few chapters we will examine the response of God's people to this new life of freedom under God.

For Consideration:

- What evidence is there that the slavery of Israel in Egypt was very harsh?
- How did God rescue His people? What did the work of God on their behalf teach Israel about God and His purpose of their lives?
- How has God revealed Himself to you? What great lessons has He been teaching you about Himself and His purpose for your life?

For Prayer:

- Take a moment to consider the goodness of the Lord toward you. Thank Him for how He has lead, protected and kept you.
- Ask the Lord to help you to learn the lessons He wants you to learn through the circumstances He brings your way.

- Ask God to teach you to be submissive to Him and to trust Him in all things.

CHAPTER 2 - LIFE IS NOT EASY

> 3 Would that we had died …when we sat by meat pots and ate bread to the full." (Exodus 16)

The people of God had been in the desert now for about two months (Exodus 16:1). It is quite likely that the excitement of being set free from their bondage and slavery was wearing off. The wilderness was not the most pleasant place to be. The scarcity of food was one of the issues they had to deal with at this time. The provisions they had brought for their journey were now likely being used up and the people began to wonder where they would find their next meal.

As their stomach's began to feel the pangs of hunger, the people became anxious. That anxiety would eventually turn to anger and resentment. In their anger, one day they came to Moses and Aaron and said: "Would that we had died… when we sat by meat pots and ate bread to the full" (Exodus 16:3).

This statement reveals something about the people of Israel and their attitude toward life in general. What were these people saying to their leaders that day? They were saying something like this: "We would rather die than not be able to sit by our meat pots and eat bread until our bellies are full."

Remember that these are former slaves speaking here. They had been used to hardships. In fact, their spirit had been broken by the harshness of their slavery. This taste of freedom, however, was creating in them a new set of ideas. They had expectations about this new-found freedom, and struggle or difficulties were not part of that idea.

They believed that if they were free now from Egypt, they should be able to have what they wanted in life. They had already endured enough hardship. Now they wanted to enjoy life. They wanted to experience life's pleasures and comforts. They wanted satisfaction and an easier lifestyle. Sacrifice and hardship were not to be part of the life of freedom they had now embarked on as a people. They fully expected that life was to be easy and comfortable now that they were no longer slaves.

The freedom they wanted was a freedom to live as they pleased. It was a freedom from want, hunger or need. They wanted a to be free from discomfort and worry. They wanted freedom from concern about their next meal. Life was to be simpler now that they were no longer slaves. The freedom they expected was quite self-centred. It was about them and their comfortable lives.

Notice from the verse that they felt so strongly about this that they told Moses and Aaron that they would rather die than live another day in want and concern. If this was freedom, they wanted nothing to do with it. What good was their freedom if they still had to suffer? Was this any different from what they were experiencing in Egypt under slavery?

Are these thoughts really all that far removed from us today? Let's consider what the Israelites are saying to their leaders here. Were they not saying to Moses that they had been expecting an easy and blessed life? There are many believers today who feel the same way. They believe that when they come to Jesus, life should be easier for them. Sometimes even in our evangelism we fall prey to this idea when we offer the unbeliever and easier life if they would only come to Jesus.

Multitudes followed the Lord Jesus when He was on this earth. Many of them followed Him for what they could get out of Him. They wanted something to eat. They wanted to be healed of their diseases and sickness. They wanted Him to be their king and overcome the oppressive Roman authorities. At the slightest hint of opposition, however, they turned away.

Jesus spoke about this kind of follower when he told a parable about a sower sowing seeds on rocky and thorny ground. Interpreting this parable, Jesus told his listeners:

> 20 As for what was sown on rocky ground, this is the one who hears the word and immediately receives it with joy, 21 yet he has no root in himself, but endures for a while, and when tribulation or persecution arises on account of the word, immediately he falls away. 22 As for what was sown among thorns, this is the one who hears the word, but the cares of the world and the deceitfulness of riches choke the word, and it proves unfruitful. (Matthew 13)

Notice that these individuals receive the word of Jesus with great joy, but when trials come their way, they fall away. These individuals believe what Israel believed—if we follow the Lord and know the freedom He brings, then things should be easier for us. Why would we follow Jesus if He does not make our life easier and more comfortable?

Israel expected ease and comfort. If they didn't have this, then they felt it would be better for them to die. If their freedom wasn't making things easier for them, there was nothing to live for.

The freedom they experienced in the wilderness was not what they expected. There was struggle in this freedom. There was hardship in this freedom. Things were not easy. They were not in control of their circumstances. They had enemies to face and many concerns. Why should they embrace this kind of freedom?

How easy it is for us to feel as Israel felt. Why would we embrace a relationship with Christ that may very well mean losing our friends? Why would we embrace a salvation that may mean risking our lives? Why should we embrace a God who may lead us from the security we find ourselves in now to a life of constant dependence?

Is our salvation and freedom really all about us and our comfort, or is it about something much greater? Why does a soldier willingly risk his or her life on the battlefield? Why does a mother delight in sacrificing her time and effort for her family? Are there not causes bigger than ourselves? The faith of Israel in the day of Moses was very selfish. It was a faith that placed themselves on the throne. Everything needed to revolve around them. Their needs and desires were to be centre stage.

God's people had forgotten the tremendous journey He was taking them on. He was ministering to them and teaching them lessons that ought to have changed their lives forever. God's purpose was far bigger than the physical hunger they felt. He was creating a nation. He was preparing them to be a great people for the glory of His name. Through them God would reveal Himself to the world.

As we examine Exodus 16:3 we begin to understand just how small our faith can be. Will you abandon a God who does not give you everything you want, when you want it? Will you turn your back on a God who allows you to face struggle and turmoil in life? Is your faith about you alone or is it far greater than this?

Will you, like many other great men and women of faith before us willingly and joyfully endure suffering and pain for the faith given you? Will you willingly sacrifice all for the Lord Jesus? Will you willingly lay down your life or will you like Esau, give up your birth right for a bowl of soup to meet your immediate need? Are there not some causes worth suffering for?

For Consideration:

- What does Exodus 16:3 tell us about Israel's attitude toward faith and life?
- Why should we embrace a faith that may lead to suffering and trial?
- What causes are worth suffering for in life?

- What causes people to turn from their faith today?
- Is there evidence of self-centred faith today? Explain.

For Prayer:

- Ask the Lord to free you from self-centredness in your faith.
- Ask the Lord to give you a better understanding of the cause you represent. Ask Him to give you a deeper passion for that cause.
- Thank the Lord for the sacrifices He was willing to make on your behalf. Ask Him to help you to be faithful despite the hardships of life.
- Have you been facing hardship and trial like Israel in this passage? Ask the Lord to provide all you need to continue faithfully with Him.

Chapter 3 -
The Unsatisfied Flesh

> ... in the land of Egypt, when we sat by the meat pots and ate bread to the full (Exodus 16:3)

In the previous chapter we examined the attitude of the people of Israel toward their new-found freedom. They wanted and expected that in this new freedom, life should be easy for them. Their faith was self-centred and they failed to see the bigger picture of what God was doing in their lives.

There is something else we need to see about Israel and her attitude at this time. This is revealed in the phrase: "in the land of Egypt, when we sat by the meat pots and ate bread to the full" The idea here is that in Egypt they had all they wanted to eat. Compared to what they were going through now, life in Egypt appeared to be very appealing.

Let's take a moment to reflect on this statement. What was life like for the children of Israel in the land of Egypt? We have already examined this in chapter 1. Exodus 2:23 tells us that they people of Israel "groaned because of their slavery and cried out for help." We read in Exodus 6:9 that the people would not even listen to Moses their deliverer "because of their broken spirit and harsh slavery." Exodus 1:13 describes the conditions under which the people of God worked:

> 13 So they ruthlessly made the people of Israel work as slaves 14 and made their lives bitter with hard service, in mortar and brick, and in all kinds of work in the field. In all their work they ruthlessly made them work as slaves. (Exodus 1)

You will also remember the decision of Pharaoh to kill every male child born to the people of Israel by throwing them in the Nile River to drown. What was it like to live in Egypt in those days? It meant harsh labour. It meant being treated ruthlessly by Egyptian taskmasters. It meant watching your young male children being drowned in the Nile River. It meant groaning under the harshness of life in bondage. It meant going to work in the fields every day with a broken spirit. In their despair, the people cried out to God for help and deliverance (Exodus 2:23). For the nation of Israel, these were days of tremendous agony.

It is for this reason that the phrase "in the land of Egypt, when we sat by meat pots and ate bread to the full," is striking. Egypt was a terrible place for Israel, and yet here they long to be back there by their meat pots eating bread until their bellies were full.

The cry of the flesh was very real for the people of Israel in this verse. Egypt, as cruel as it was, did offer its pleasures. For a moment, as they ate their bread and enjoyed their meat, the pain of their slavery disappeared. It never left them, however, for when they got up from eating they were faced with the harshness of their conditions. Their bread was but a momentary relief but their agony continued. Egypt offered pleasurable experiences but always behind that pleasure was the bondage of slavery and oppression. Their bellies were full but their souls remained in turmoil.

As Israel wondered where the next meal was going to come from in the desert, their minds returned to Egypt and the temporary pleasures she had offered. Israel wasn't seeing the big picture, however. She was only seeing the bread and the meat that temporarily filled her belly. She wasn't seeing the agony of soul and despair that Egypt brought with that bread.

In Genesis 25:29-34 Esau came in from the field exhausted and asked his brother Jacob for some stew. Jacob would only give him this stew if he sold him his birth right. Esau agreed. To fill his hunger, Esau was willing to sacrifice his rights as the eldest child. I do not want to depreciate the significance of hunger here. What I do want to communicate, however, is how easy it is for us to feed the cravings of the flesh without considering the consequences. As Israel travelled through the wilderness, God was taking her to the Promises Land. Here, however, she was willing to give up the Promised Land for the cost of her next meal.

The pull of the flesh is incredibly strong, especially in moments of weakness and trial. It is easy to lose touch with reality. Here we see Israel longing for Egypt, the place of bondage and cruel oppression, just to have assurance of the next meal. Satan is a master at blinding us to the consequences of our actions. Genesis 3:2-6 is a clear example of this:

> 2 And the woman said to the serpent, "We may eat
> of the fruit of the trees in the garden, 3 but God
> said, "You shall not eat of the fruit of the tree that
> is in the midst of the garden, neither shall you touch
> it, lest you die." 4 But the serpent said to the
> woman, "You will not surely die. 5 For God knows
> that when you eat of it your eyes will be opened,
> and you will be like God, knowing good and evil." 6
> So when the woman saw that the tree was good for
> food, and that it was a delight to the eyes, and that
> the tree was to be desired to make one wise, she
> took of its fruit and ate, and she also gave some to
> her husband who was with her, and he ate. (Genesis 3)

God's warning to Adam and Eve was that they would die if they ate the fruit from a certain tree. Satan, however, showed them that it was tasty fruit, and would open their eyes to a whole new world. That world, however, was a world of sin and death, just as the Lord God had described. The pull of the flesh was so strong that for the taste of the fruit from that tree, Eve surrendered to sin and death.

The meat pots and bread of Egypt will always be a temptation to the hungry flesh. In Israel's trial, the flesh began to cry out very loudly. Like Esau, she would have given up the Promised Land to be back in Egypt eating bread. The path to the Promised Land was not going to be easy.

There will be times when we, too, will feel the pangs of hunger. We may be tempted, like Israel, to look back and remember the things we enjoyed in the past, when certain things in life were easier. Egypt did offer pleasures to God's people, but those pleasures came at a great cost.

The path to the promised land took the Children of Israel through the wilderness with all its struggles. Our journeys in life will also take us through wilderness experiences. For those moments of struggle, however, we gain eternal joy. Will we sacrifice the purpose of God to sit by the meat pots of Egypt? As you face the temptations and trials before you, recognise the pull of the flesh. Recognise also that there are some things that are worth suffering and waiting for. The pleasures of Egypt cannot compare to what God has promised. Great blessings come through sacrifice.

Let us never underestimate the pull of the unsatisfied flesh. The temptation to satisfy the needs of the moment will be very real for us as well. May God give us grace, however, to recognize the cost of satisfying those fleshly desires in an ungodly way. The flesh cries in all of us. The need for companionship, provision, protection, satisfaction, assurance, comfort and love all cry out in us. Israel's need was a legitimate one. She needed to eat and satisfy her physical hunger. The problem was that she did not seem to be able to commit this need to the Lord and trust Him with it. Can you trust the Lord with the unsatisfied needs? The God who heard the cry of the people of Israel in their bondage is the same God who brought them out into the wilderness. He would provide for their every need. For the moment, however, the cry of the flesh became Israel's god. When it spoke, they followed. Instead of committing this need to God, they followed its impulses, longed for Egypt.

Many before us have fallen because they listened to the cry of their flesh rather than to God. David committed adultery because of the call of the flesh. He would also stoop to murder to cover his sin. Eve sold herself to Satan for a taste of fruit from the Tree of the Knowledge of Good and

Evil. Esau gave up his birth right for a pot of stew. Cain would kill his brother Abel to satisfy the jealous anger of his fleshly heart. The flesh must never become our master and god. It must be held in subjection to the higher purpose of God for our lives.

As we face the wilderness of life, the flesh will cry out in us for satisfaction. It will long for Egypt. It will remind us of the pleasures of past days. Its passions and desires, however, must be brought to God and surrendered to Him. As we look at the story of Israel in those days, we see how God met their need on a daily basis in wonderful and miraculous ways. We have every reason to believe that He will do the same for us as we trust in Him and surrender to His purposes rather than to the pull of our flesh.

For Consideration:

- What was the land of Egypt like for the people of God?
- What does this verse teach us about the pull of the flesh? Have you ever felt that pull?
- How does Satan blind us to the bigger picture and the results of our actions and desires?
- Have you ever found yourself being tempted to surrender to the lusts and desires of the flesh? What do you think would be the end result of such a surrender?
- Are you willing to endure the hardships of the wilderness for the promises of God?

For Prayer:

- Thank the Lord for delivering you from the bondage of sin.

- Ask God to help you to surrender the desires of your flesh to Him. Thank Him that He is not opposed to those desires but wants to fulfil them in His way.

- Ask God to help you to see the big picture. Ask Him to give you strength to endure and resist the temptations of the flesh so that you can experience the promises of God.

- Ask God to give you the ability to resist making the desires of the flesh gods your life. Commit yourself afresh to honour God in your body and mind.

Chapter 4 - The Harshness of the Healing

> 3 Would that we had died by the hand of the Lord in the land of Egypt ... for you have brought us out into this wilderness to kill this assembly... (Exodus 16)

So far in Exodus 16:3 we have seen the mentality in Israel that life should have been easy now that they were free from the bondage of Egypt. They were very disappointed that this was not always the case. Then we saw the incredible pull of the flesh and Israel's desire to satisfy its cravings. These two facts alone were tools in the hand of the enemy to tempt them to give up hope of the Promised Land to which they were heading. There was, however, evidence of yet another misunderstanding in the minds of the people of God. This is found in the phrase, "would that we had died by the hand of the Lord in the land of Egypt... for you have brought us out into this wilderness to kill this assembly." Let's break these words down.

As we begin notice that there is a comparison between God and Moses in the phrase— "would that we had died by the hand of the Lord... but you (speaking of Moses) have brought us out into the wilderness to kill this assembly." The people of Israel say here that it would have been preferable for them to die at the hands of God rather than at to die under the leadership of Moses. Notice that in both cases they speak about dying.

Israel understood the struggles of Egypt and that she would likely have perished under its bondage. They believed, however, that this death at the hands of the Lord in Egypt, would have been more compassionate than what was happening to them now under the leadership of Moses. The accused Moses of taking them into the wilderness to kill them with hunger. God would have at least allowed them to die with a full stomach.

While it is true that the Lord God we serve is a compassionate and loving God, we often misunderstand the meaning of compassion. Was the Lord God compassionate when He allowed His Son Jesus to die the cruel death of the cross? Was the death of the Lord Jesus not the measure of true compassion? As cruel and as difficult as this was, it was the means of our salvation.

Is the doctor compassionate when he cuts open the body of a patient, inflicting it with pain, in order to heal the deeper sickness of the body? Is a parent compassionate with he or she disciplines his or her child in order to keep them on the path of life and faith? Compassion is not always easy. Sometimes the compassionate thing to do will hurt the one you love in order to keep them from even more pain and devastation.

Israel believed that God would have been more gentle with them. He would not have allowed them to die with an empty stomach in the middle of a hot desert. What they failed to see was that the God they spoke about had led them step by step to this place. In this time of trouble, they blamed Moses for their problems.

A number of years ago I was leading a Bible Study on the island of Reunion in the Indian Ocean. I can't remember the passage we were examining but I do recall the response of one of the ladies in the group. She had been in a conversation with a sister in Christ who told her that she could not believe in a Jesus that did not heal. As she shared this conversation with us, I remember her telling the Bible study group how, after reflecting on what her friend had said, she came to the conclusion that she would believe in Jesus whether He healed or not?

That statement touched me in a powerful way. I believe in a Jesus who heals, but what if He doesn't heal me? Would I still believe in Him? An acquaintance of mine is a man who was born blind. He told me that he had often sought the Lord for healing but the Lord never gave him that healing. He is a man of tremendous faith and trust in the Lord. He continues to serve the Lord with great joy and enthusiasm, despite his blindness. He believes in Jesus whether he is healed of his blindness or not.

Consider the Old Testament saint, Job. On one occasion Satan came to God and asked permission to strip him of his health and possessions. God granted that permission. With this permission granted by God, Satan went out to kill Job's children. He also afflicted Job with painful boils. (see Job 1,2). In the end even Job's wife pleaded with her husband to curse God and die. Listen to his response:

> 9 Then his wife said to him, “Do you still hold fast your integrity? Curse God and die.” 10 But he said to her, “You speak as one of the foolish women would speak. Shall we receive good from God, and shall we not receive evil?” In all this Job did not sin with his lips. (Job 2)

Job accepted his pain as being from the Lord. He did not understand it, but He was willing to accept it. How many of us have stood by the beds of those we loved and watched them die? Somehow we believe that God would never take away a loved one from us. We cannot accept a God who would allow anything bad to happen.

Admittedly, the trials of Job were inflicted upon Him by Satan, but remember that God allowed Satan to do this to His servant. Will you believe in a God who allows hard things in life? Will you believe in a God who does not allow a friend to be healed of his blindness?

One day the apostle Paul approached the Lord about an affliction he had in his flesh. He prayed that the Lord would remove this “thorn.” Listen to the response of the Lord:

> 8 Three times I pleaded with the Lord about this, that it should leave me. 9 But he told me, “My grace is sufficient for you, for my power is made perfect in weakness.” Therefore, I will boast all the more gladly of my weaknesses, so that the power of Christ may rest upon me. (2 Corinthians 12)

Paul experienced the wonderful power of God because of that weakness. God allowed him to suffer so that he would be able to trust all the more in Him and His enabling in ministry and life. This ultimately made Paul the man he was.

As an oyster feeds on the bottom of the sea, sometimes a grain of sand will get lodged inside its body. This grain of sand is an irritation to the oyster. To protect itself from this constant irritation, the oyster will secrete a calcium carbonate based substance called nacre. As long as that grain of sand remains in the body of the oyster, it will I continue to secrete this nacre. The result of these layers of secretion is the pearl which is widely sought after and prized. For this pearl to be formed, the oyster had to be irritated. This is what was happening in the life of Paul. This is what was happening in the life of Israel in Exodus 16:3. God had allowed irritation in their lives to form in them the precious qualities He needed.

Israel's view of God was that He would be compassionate. They had a hard time believing that God would allow hardships like the ones they were experiencing that day. This kept them from seeing His greater work in their lives. Their God was a God of love, gentleness and compassion. He always satisfied their needs and never allowed anything too difficult in their lives. They failed to see that there were times when they needed to be stretched in their faith. They failed to see that God needed to place irritations in their lives to shape them into the people they needed to be.

Yes, God is a God of tremendous compassion and mercy. He is a God, however, who is more concerned for our growth and maturity in Him than in our temporary comforts. He will allow struggles to come our way, using those struggles to shape and mould us into His image. Through those struggles we will be drawn closer to Him.

Israel could not accept their trial as being from God. They blamed Moses for this because they felt that the God they served would never have allowed them to face this kind of hunger and uncertainty. If we cannot accept our circumstances as either being from God or allowed by God for our good, we will miss out on the blessings that those trials are intended to bring. Satan delights to tell us that a good and loving God would never allow us to face uncertainty or struggle in life. I have met many who have believed this lie. I have also seen them wander from God as a result.

Israel could not believe in a God who would not satisfy their hunger. Will you believe whether He meets your need or not? Will you trust Him even when you do not understand or like what He is doing? Sometimes the healing is harsh. Be assured that however harsh that healing appears to be, that it is in the hands of God, who is concerned for your ultimate well-being and growth.

For Consideration:

- What does this verse teach us about Israel's view of God?
- Does God always make things comfortable and easy for us?
- What does God accomplish in us through the trials and difficulties He allows?
- How does belief in a God that only works for my comfort and ease keep me from maturing in my spiritual life?
- Can you trust a God who allows struggles and difficulties in your life?

- What struggles has God allowed you to face in life? How have these difficulties helped you to grow in your relationship with Him?

For Prayer:

- Take a moment to thank the Lord for the blessings He has given you through the difficult times in your life? Thank Him for how He has used those difficult times to mature you in your faith and walk with Him.

- Ask the Lord to give you grace to accept the things He allows to come your way.

- Do you have a friend or loved one who is struggling right now? Ask the Lord to bless and keep them in this time.

- Ask the Lord to give you faith to trust Him in whatever situation you find yourself today.

Chapter 5 - The People in My Life

> For you have brought us out into the wilderness (Exodus 16:3)

In the last chapter we saw that the Lord God sometimes allows trials in our live. These trials are not out of His control, but used by God to accomplish His purpose. As Job and Paul accepted the afflictions and thorns in their lives, they were refined and drawn closer to God. They would ultimately become more effective servants of God because of those struggles.

I would like to develop this thought one step further in this chapter. As the people of God wandered in the wilderness, they began to feel the stress of that journey. They began to wonder where their next meal was going to come from and how they were going to survive as a people in this inhospitable environment.

In response these concerns the people of Israel cried out to Moses in the words we have quoted at the beginning of this chapter: "you have brought us out into this wilderness to kill this whole assembly with hunger" (Exodus 16:3).

What is important for us to note here in this statement is that the people were speaking to Moses and Aaron as their leaders. They accused these men of bringing them out into the wilderness. They blamed their leaders for their circumstances. Under the leadership of Moses and Aaron in Egypt they had seen incredible miracles taking place. The nation of Egypt was brought to its knees as a result of the work of God through these two men.

They watched as Moses raised his staff over the Red Sea to drown the pursuing Egyptian army. They were willing to put their confidence in Moses because of the great signs that had taken place through him. When things did not go as they anticipated, however, they were also very quick to speak out against the servants of God.

Notice particularly that the people blamed Moses and Aaron for bringing them out into this wilderness. Admittedly, Moses and Aaron were their leaders, but what the people of God failed to appreciate at this time was that their leaders were instruments in the hands of God. Ultimately, it was not Moses who brought them out into the wilderness but the Lord God. He was the power behind Moses. He was the one who broke the back of Egypt so that His people could be freed from bondage. He was the one who empowered Moses to lead His people.

The Lord God led His people through the wilderness by means of a pillar of cloud and fire. The people would only move as that pillar moved.

> 18 At the command of the Lord the people of Israel
> set out, and at the command of the Lord they
> camped. As long as the cloud rested over the tab-
> ernacle, they remained in camp. 19 Even when the
> cloud continued over the tabernacle many days the

> people of Israel kept the charge of the Lord and did
> not set out. 20 Sometimes the cloud was a few
> days over the tabernacle, and according to the
> command of the Lord they remained in camp; then
> according to the command of the Lord they set out.
> 21 And sometimes the cloud remained from even-
> ing until morning, and when the cloud lifted in the
> morning, they set out, or if it continued for a day
> and a night, when the cloud lifted they set out. 22
> Whether it was two days, or a month, or a longer
> time, that the cloud continued over the tabernacle,
> abiding there, the people remained in camp and did
> not set out, but when it lifted they set out. (Numbers
> 9:18-22)

Moses were merely a servant of the Lord. The cloud of God had led them to the very place they found themselves now. They had followed that cloud to this exact spot. When the people of God were in Egypt they cried out to the Lord for deliverance. The Lord answered that prayer by sending Moses and Aaron. Their prayer had been answered but not in the way Israel had anticipated.

Israel wasn't sure they liked Moses and Aaron as their leaders. Deep down they understood that God had led them to this place in the desert but they somehow believed Moses was to stand up for them and defend them against these uncomfortable ways. When things didn't go the way they wanted, they blamed Moses.

The people of Israel began to see Moses as their servant and not the servant of God. I have seen this often in churches of our day. I have seen pastors choosing to be servants of people rather than servants of God. They compromise the message the Lord has given them for the people and make it more pleasant to the ears. They only tell people what they want to hear. These are not true servants of God. Moses was leading the people as God had determined. This brought him into conflict with the people. By grumbling against Moses they were grumbling against the purpose of God for their good. Their complaint was not really with Moses but with God.

The apostle Paul knew the difference between seeking to gain the approval of man and pleasing God when he wrote:

> 10 For am I now seeking the approval of man, or of God? Or am I trying to please man? If I were still trying to please man, I would not be a servant of Christ. (Galatians 1)

Being a servant of God will not bring us popularity. Moses was accused of bringing his people into the desert to kill them with hunger. His efforts were not appreciated. God's true servants are not commissioned by God to make everything easy and comfortable. They will speak things to us we don't want to hear. They will challenge us in ways we do not want to be counselled. They will lead us into places we do not always want to go. If they are true servants of God, however, the represent Him and His purpose for our lives.

The people God chooses to bless us and partner with us on the journey of life will not always be what we anticipate. Are you married to a partner who is very different from you? Do you work with people who see things very differently? Are there people in your church who have different priorities in life? Israel expected a different style of leader and often complained and grumbled about Moses. Instead of submitting, they resisted. In their resistance they missed out on the blessing of God.

In our lives we will often encounter people who are different from us. Sometimes these people are the instruments of God to refine us. We can resist them and complain about them or we can learn to work with them and allow God to change us through them.

When the people of Israel were taken into captivity in Babylon, the prophet Jeremiah spoke to them saying:

> 4 "Thus says the Lord of hosts, the God of Israel, to all the exiles whom I have sent into exile from Jerusalem to Babylon: 5 Build houses and live in them; plant gardens and eat their produce. 6 Take wives and have sons and daughters; take wives for your sons, and give your daughters in marriage, that they may bear sons and daughters; multiply there, and do not decrease. 7 But seek the welfare of the city where I have sent you into exile, and pray to the Lord on its behalf, for in its welfare you will find your welfare. (Jeremiah 29)

The circumstances and people God brings on our path may not be what we want in life. In Jeremiah 29 the people of God were in exile with a foreign leadership over them. Their natural tendency was to grumble and complain. God told them through Jeremiah to plant gardens, give their sons and daughters in marriage and to seek the welfare of the city of their exile. He told the people that the welfare of the city to which they were exiled would also be their welfare.

In Exodus 16:3 we see the people of God grumbling against Moses. As much as the people disliked him, Moses was the man God had chosen to be their leader. He would be the one God would use to bring them to the land

He promised their fathers and mothers. God's servants are not always what we expect, nor are His ways.

Like Israel, we can grumble and complain about the people God brings our way. From Israel's perspective, Moses was only leading them into danger and death. But Moses, however much disliked by the people of Israel, was the man of God for the hour. He was God's choice to bring His people into the Land of Promise.

We can so easily grumble about God's methods and the people He chooses to use. David, before becoming king of Israel, was constantly pursued by jealous Saul. He had opportunities to kill Saul and remove this threat, but he chose to respect him as the king God had chosen over Israel. We do not know what these times of hiding and running from Saul accomplished in the life of David. One thing is clear, however—David would become one of the greatest kings Israel ever know. Somehow, his willingness to accept his difficulties at the hand of Saul would play a role in making him the king he would prove to be.

What kind of people has God brought into your life? As human beings all of them are flawed. They may, also, however, prove to be the very people needed to refine you and make you into everything God intends you to be. May God give us grace to accept the people He brings into our lives. May He teach us through them and use them to make us the people He is proud to call His own.

For Consideration:

- What evidence do we have in the history of Israel that the Lord God was the One who was leading them through the wilderness?
- What was the expectation of the people of Israel toward Moses as their leader? What do we expect of our leaders?
- What is the temptation in leadership to give people what they want and to be popular with the people around us? How does this lead to compromise?
- Are there people in your life you find difficult to work with? What has been your response to those people?
- What it the challenge of this passage in dealing with difficult people?

For Prayer:

- Take a moment to recognise before the Lord that His ways are often different from ours and that the people He chooses to use in our lives are often different from what we expect.
- Ask God to give you grace to accept the people and circumstances He has brought your way. Thank Him that He is able to use them to refine us and make us into the people He wants us to be.
- Ask God to keep you from grumbling and complaining about the things you do not understand or like.

Ask Him to give you grace to trust Him in the difficulties you find yourself in today.

Chapter 6 -
Faith in God's Purpose

> "You have brought us into the wilderness to kill this assembly with hunger." (Exodus 16:3)

There is one more detail I would like to touch on here in this verse. In the last chapter we saw how the prayers of God's servants were not answered in the way they had anticipated. After being released from bondage they found themselves in the desert, uncertain about where the next meal was going to come from.

Remember that these were the people who had just been released from Egypt. There in the land of Egypt they had seen the Lord do incredible things. The plagues He sent had brought this most powerful nation to its knees. They watched the power of God in those days open the Red Sea to deliver them from the hands of the Egyptian army. They saw the pillar of cloud and fire in the sky each day directing them toward the Promised Land.

It was hard for Israel to imagine being freed from the oppression of Egypt, but there they were. Their chains were gone. The whips were gone. The forced labour had ended. They were free! Their God had delivered them.

Standing now, however, facing hunger and worry, they spoke out against Moses, accusing him of bringing them out into the wilderness to kill them with hunger. Consider this in the context of what God had been doing. When they cried out to Him for deliverance from their slavery, the Lord God came to their rescue and miraculously set them free (Exodus 2:23-24). When they cried out to Him as the army of Egypt approached, God opened the waters of the Red Sea for them (Exodus 14). As they left the land of Egypt, the Egyptians –their cruel enemies, showered them with blessings and gifts for the journey (Exodus 12:35-36). In Marah, when the water was so bitter they could not drink it, the Lord sweetened the water to provide for their thirst (Exodus 15:22-27). These circumstances proved that their God was with them and would provide for their need.

Have you ever wondered why we never seem to learn from past experiences? We see God provide and when we come to another test of our faith we again begin to worry. There is something about human nature that wants to be in control and understand our circumstances. When we find ourselves in situations where we are no longer in control we begin to worry and fret. Israel was in such a situation. They could not possibly see where their next meal was going to come from. There were likely over two million people on this journey and the desert was a barren place. Human reason told them that they were in a very difficult situation and unless they did something about it quickly they would surely perish. Consider the following quote:

> Dr. Danny Kellum, Headmaster of Donelson Christian Academy, wrote:

"One of the biggest arithmetical miracles in the world: Moses and the people were in the desert, but what was he going to do with them? They had to be fed, and feeding 3 or 3 1/2 million people requires a lot of food.

According to the Quartermaster General in the Army, it is reported that Moses would have to have 1,500 tons of food each day. Do you know that to bring that much food each day, two freight trains each a mile long would be required!

Besides you must remember, they were out in the desert, and they would have to have firewood to use in cooking the food. This would take 4,000 tons of wood and a few more freight trains each a mile long, just for one day.

And just think, they were forty years in transit.

Oh, yes, they would have to have water. If they only had enough to drink and wash a few dishes, it would take 11,000,000 gallons each day, and a freight train with tank cars 1,800 miles long, just to bring water!

And then another thing. They had to get across the Red Sea at night. Now, if they went on a narrow path, double file, the line would be 800 miles long and would require 35 days and nights to get through. So, there had to be a space in the Red Sea, 3 miles wide so that they could walk 5,000 abreast to get over in one night.

> But then another problem. Each time they camped at the end of the day, a campground two-thirds the size of the state of Rhode Island was required, or a total of 750 square miles long, think of it! This space just for nightly camping.
>
> Do you think Moses figured all this out before he left Egypt? I think not! You see, Moses believed in God. God took care of these things for him.
>
> (http://www.kubik.org/lighter/exodus.htm)

Logically, there was no way for the people of Israel to survive in the wilderness. God, however, is beyond human logic. His ways are different from our ways. He is the God of the impossible. Israel was not seeing this right now. All they could see was the facts and statistics. Israel's mind could not comprehend how they could survive another day. From their human perspective, they were all going to perish in the wilderness. There was no hope of ever getting to the Promised Land.

Have you ever found yourself in the situation the people of Israel were in? You look at your circumstances and think you could not survive another day. Your mind is not able to imagine how you could ever get through this maze of problems and obstacles. You lose hope and surrender to what you believe is inevitable.

Imagine Moses as the leader of these people. What could he answer them when they came asking for their next meal? He did not have anything to offer. He was helpless in himself to provide. God alone was able. But He was the God who was leading them. He was the God of the impossible. While things were beyond them, they were not beyond this great God of the impossible.

As Moses himself wondered how the Lord would provide for these people, God spoke to Him: "Behold, I am about to rain bread from heaven for you..." (Exodus 16:4). In fact, for forty years, God would rain down this bread from heaven—one day's supply at a time. Every morning they awoke and looked out of their tent there before them was the manna for the day. Any time they gathered more than a day's supply, what was left over spoiled (except for the Sabbath supply which lasted for two days). Through this means, God kept His people in constant daily dependence.

The people of Israel in Exodus 16 were looking at matters from a human perspective. Yes, things were impossible from this perspective. They failed to look to God, however. They failed to see that He had provided for them in the past and would continue to do so in the future. He would provide everything they needed one day at a time.

It is true that many of those who left Egypt would perish in the wilderness, but it was not from hunger but because of their grumbling and constant disobedience. They would not die for lack of provision but for their distrust in God and His purpose.

As often as I have seen the Lord provide, I find still in my heart the same tendency I see in Israel. "We're going to die. There is no way we are going to get through this wilderness." Then I realise that there is a God in heaven who has led me to this place. It is an uncomfortable place but it is for my good. The One who has brought me here will either lead me out or give me grace for each day to live in hope and victory.

Do you find yourself with the attitude of Israel here in Exodus 16:3? Lift up your eyes and see this God in heaven.

He will rain down bread from heaven for your daily need. You may not be able to see past that one day but you can be assured that as you place your confidence and faith in Him, He will provide all you need to live each day in His grace and provision.

For Consideration:

- How had God proven His provision and protection to Israel prior to Exodus 16:3? How has the Lord provided and protected you in the past?
- What is the difference between human wisdom and faith? How does Exodus 16:3 demonstrate a lack of faith?
- How much provision would have been necessary for the people of God in the wilderness? Can you trust God for your needs?
- God provided the needs of His people in the wilderness one day at a time. Can you accept this daily provision? Why do was seem to need more assurance than one day at a time?

For Prayer:

- Take a moment to recognise and thank the Lord for His provision and protection in your life.
- Ask the Lord to teach you to live by faith in Him and His purpose. Ask Him to give you grace not to be disheartened by human wisdom and appearances.

- Thank the Lord that He provides all we need for what He calls us to do. Commit your need to Him and ask Him to give you patience and faith to trust Him for the answers.

- Thank the Lord for his strength and provision for you today. Thank Him that you can be confident of His grace for each day of your life.

Chapter 7 - Conclusion and Application

To be honest with you, when I felt the Lord put Exodus 16:3 on my heart to study, I wasn't sure where He wanted me to go with it. Each day I came to reflect on the passage He showed me yet another aspect to the verse. Let's conclude our reflection by summarising what we have seen and tying the last six chapters together.

The Context

The context of Exodus 16:3 is one of suffering and confusion. God's people had just been set free from the bondage of Egypt, but now they faced the uncertainty of the desert. Humanly speaking they could not see how they could survive in this inhospitable climate. Their freedom from slavery did not mean freedom from problems in life. This perplexed them.

The Question

The question this verse makes us ask is this: "What does freedom and blessing look like in the Christian life?" There are many who come to the Lord expecting that everything will be perfect. They are surprised to find that they still have deep hurts and problems in life. Like the children of Israel, they begin to wonder why they are serving the Lord when the life of service is just as hard as the life of bondage.

God doesn't call us to a life of ease. He calls us to a life of trust and purpose. He gives us a purpose worth suffering for. If we reduce life to ease and comfort, we miss out on the greatest blessing. Many have died without hope and purpose in a life of ease and comfort. Those who suffer and die with a purpose, however, are truly blessed. God wants to give us purpose.

Some years ago I was in Haiti. As I looked around me and saw the tremendous needs I asked myself what I was doing to ease this suffering. As I reflected on the call of God to teach His Word I felt a little guilty and wondered what teaching the Word had to do with the tremendous physical and emotional suffering I saw around me. When I spoke to the Lord about this I sensed Him say to me: "Wayne, people need more than to survive, they also need a reason to live. Write to give them that purpose." Those words have always remained with me. God wants to give us a that reason to live. Struggle and pain are the fruit of a sinful world. We will not be free of afflictions until we enter God's Promised Land. God, however, will give us a reason to live that will carry us through those difficulties and problems. True blessing in the Christian life is not about a trouble-free life but about a purpose to live despite the pain of a sinful world.

The Temptation

As we live in this world, the pull of our flesh and its desires will be a real test for us. Unfulfilled needs and desires will be one of our greatest struggles. These desire will cry out to be satisfied, whether they be physical or emotional. In the case of Israel, the hunger in their belly was such that they wanted to go back to Egypt—the land of bondage and slavery.

Life, however, is not about pleasing the flesh or our emotions. The flesh is not always right. Sometimes true purpose and contentment comes from denying the pull of the flesh for something greater. Many have satisfied the burning desires of the flesh and emotions only to find that things got worse for them. The unleashing of anger or bitterness did not bring them the victory they wanted. They satisfaction of their physical desires only led them to become hopelessly entrapped.

Our physical needs must be submitted to the Lord. The attitudes of the mind must be surrendered to the purpose of His will. This will require dying to the flesh and its intense desires to do what it right before God. This was something Israel struggled with in Exodus 16. The pull of the flesh was a real temptation.

Athletes know that if they are going to win the race, they must learn to discipline or deny the flesh. This means taking charge of their body to make it do what needs to be done to win the race. The Christian life is no different. The temptations of the flesh and mind must be surrendered to the greater will of God. This means looking beyond the physical needs to the purpose of God in life. It means being willing to deny ourselves and the cry of the flesh for revenge. The temptations of the flesh and mind must be overcome if we are to walk in victory. The flesh is not always right.

Our Concept of God

As Israel wandered through the desert they had to learn about the God who was leading them. They saw their God as a servant whose duty it was to minister to their every need. When they were thirsty, He was to provide water. When they needed help, He was to rush to their aid. When they were hungry, He was to supply food.

This attitude still is evident in our day. The God of many is not God but a servant. His duty is only to cater to the needs of His people. In fact, as servant, He is less than His people. This is not the God we serve. The God of the Bible is a Sovereign and Holy God who deserves respect and honour. He is not a servant of humanity, although He does minister to our every need. He willingly offers Himself to be our God and to bless, but He is not our servant; He is our gracious and compassionate Lord who deserves our obedience and reverence.

We dare not reduce the God of the Bible to servant. His concern is not so much about our temporary comfort as our intimacy with Him. Parents will need to discipline their children. Teachers will need to challenge their students to new heights if they are to learn. Coaches will need to push the athletes they train to endure pain for long term gain. To say that God is all about my comfort is to misrepresent Him.

Will God allow us to go through difficult times? Sure He will? All this, however, is for our good. He will use what we face to shape us into the people we need to be. God is not focused on our comfort and ease, His desire is for our growth and maturity. Israel struggled with this lesson.

The Ways of God

God's ways are not our ways. Israel prayed to God when she was in her bondage and asked Him to set her free. God sent Moses. Moses was the man they had rejected some forty years earlier. He was not the one they had anticipated.

God's ways are often strange to us. Sometimes the very people you struggle with are the people God wants to use in your life. These people will refine you and shape your life. The circumstances God places you in will be tools in His hands to change your life. These people and circumstances are not what we expected as the answer to our prayer, but God's doesn't do things the way we think He should. He has a greater purpose in mind.

Israel's response was to grumble against Moses. They didn't like the servant God sent. They didn't like the answer God gave. They complained and argued with God. They rejected the very instrument God wanted to use to mature and refine them.

In later years, the Lord Jesus would come to this earth to die for the sins of the world. Many who met Him in person did not see in Him the answer to the problem of sin. They rejected and crucified Him on the cross. His death, however, would be the solution of God for the problem of humanity. Will we reject what God brings for our deliverance and freedom simply because it is not what we expected?

God works in ways that are often strange to us. Let Him do His work. Accept His purpose. Let Him answer in the way that He sees best for us. Surrender to that answer and watch how He uses this strange means to bring you the victory you need.

The Faith Required

Finally, we saw how the people of Israel in Exodus 16:3 lacked the faith in God necessary to live in victory. They couldn't possibly see how God was going to provide for their needs. Sometimes God places us in impossible situations to show us what is possible.

As you live out your Christian life, you will find yourself in situations where you do not have the provision or strength necessary to carry on. In those times we allow our human wisdom to take over instead of waiting on God and trusting His strength and provision. God would provide for His people on a daily basis for over forty years. Never once would they lack the provision of God but they never had a supply of food beyond what was necessary for that day. This kept Israel dependant on God for each day.

God gives us strength and wisdom for each day. Many of us want to see the whole picture. We can't step out in faith until we understand how we are going to be able to achieve our results. We plan and double check our figures to be sure that we have all we need before stepping out. Israel did not have this privilege. As God led her through the wilderness by means of the pillar of cloud and fire, all she had was the food for the day. She was dependant on God for tomorrow.

How real is God to you? Is He concerned for you and your needs? Is He able to provide the strength, wisdom, patience, and resources you need for today? Can you trust Him and His leading? Can you wait on Him each day? When you get up in the morning can you say, "Lord, I need your wisdom for this day"? Can you trust Him for the strength you need?

Faith is not concerned about what I can do but about what God can do through the circumstances and trials that come my way. We feel like we need have to have all the answers –God is calling us to trust in Him instead for He has the answers. We feel like we need to have all the strength—God is asking us to wait on Him for the strength. Faith takes its eyes off what I can do and looks to God and what He can do through our circumstances.

Israel, in Exodus 16, lacked this faith. She grumbled and complained because she could not see how she could ever get out of her situation alive. She would have been right to be concerned about this if she had no God. The reality was, however, that Israel's God was not like them. What was impossible to Israel was possible for God. What made no sense to the Israelite mind, made perfect sense to God. Can you trust God for your situation even when it is not what you expected?

For Consideration:

- What is the difference between a life of comfort and a life of purpose?

- Have you ever felt the pull of the flesh to wander from the purpose of God? How is the flesh a temptation to us? Can we trust the flesh and its impulses?

- Is God primarily concerned about our comfort? What is He concerned about?

- How are God's ways different from ours? Do His ways always make sense to the human mind?

- What is faith? Is human wisdom enough in this life? How does faith take us where human wisdom cannot go?

For Prayer:

- Ask the Lord to give you a life of purpose. Ask Him to help you to be willing to endure the trials and struggles of this life for Him and that purpose.

- Ask God to give you grace to live a life of sacrifice and discipline. Ask Him to enable you to surrender the impulses of the flesh to Him and His purpose as found in the Word of God.

- Thank the Lord that His ways a different than ours. Ask Him for the faith necessary to believe in what He is doing even though it does not make sense to our human mind.

- Thank the Lord that His purposes are for our good.

Light To My Path Book Distribution

Light To My Path Book Distribution (LTMP) is a book writing and distribution ministry reaching out to needy Christian workers in Asia, Latin America, and Africa. Many Christian workers in developing countries do not have the resources necessary to obtain Bible training or purchase Bible study materials for their ministries and personal encouragement. F. Wayne Mac Leod is a member of Action International Ministries and has been writing these books with a goal to distribute them freely or at cost price to needy pastors and Christian workers around the world.

These books are being used in preaching, teaching, evangelism and encouragement of local believers in over sixty countries. Books have now been translated into a number of languages. The goal is to make them available to as many believers as possible.

The ministry of LTMP is a faith based ministry and we trust the Lord for the resources necessary to distribute the books for the encouragement and strengthening of believers around the world. Would you pray that the Lord would open doors for the translation and further distribution of these books? For more information about Light To My Path Book Distribution visit our website at http://ltmp-homepage.blogspot.ca

40949403R00035

Made in the USA
Lexington, KY
03 June 2019